THE
RIGHT
LADDER

THE RIGHT LADDER

Climb to your perfect career in **4** simple steps!

SIERRA MODRO

BOUND
PUBLISHING

Bound Publishing

United States
6501 E. Greenway Pkwy
#103-480
Scottsdale, AZ
85254

Canada
Suite 114
720 28th St. NE
Calgary, AB T2A 6R3

Toll Free Phone and Fax: 1-888-237-1627
Email: info@boundpublishing.com
Web: www.boundpublishing.com

ISBN (softcover): 978-0-9867762-2-9

Cover: Lloyd Arbour, www.tablloyd.com
Text: Lloyd Arbour, www.tablloyd.com
Edit:
Back cover photo: ©2011 Brian Geraths - www.yourprints.com

DEDICATION

To my husband David,
who helped me make my own LEAP

TABLE OF CONTENTS

FOREWORD

By Todd Dean, Dean Global Group

I went through a professional crisis a couple of years ago that left me unemployed and broke. At the time I felt absolutely crushed. I thought I had lost the dream – a well-paying career that allowed me to buy all the things in life that were supposed to make me happy.

Unbeknownst to me, losing my job was the best possible thing that could have happened. I hated that job. I just didn't know it. In order to mask my dissatisfaction at work I bought houses and expensive cars. I went on luxurious trips, all in an effort to buy my way out of facing the truth – what I did to make a living was destroying my enjoyment of life. On the outside, I had everything we're told we need to be fulfilled. I was admired for my prestigious position. My salary allowed for a lifestyle of luxury. If I wasn't happy, it was obviously a deeply personal reason, unsolvable by any outward changes.

After I became unemployed, I allowed myself a year off so I could take a breath and reevaluate what it was I really wanted to do with my life. Once again, I was answering that age-old question, what do you want to be when you grow up? Although I didn't know it at the time, I was using Sierra's LEAP system to envision my next career. I realized I hadn't even paused between my college graduation from Journalism and my leap into sales. Losing my job allowed me to go back to square one, a scary place to be perhaps, but a very exciting one as well. I combined my passion for media and my skills in sales and formed my own company, the Dean Global Group, which deals in radio, publishing, PR and marketing.

I met Sierra when she approached me with the idea for *The Right Ladder.* I was thrilled to be part of a project that could offer guidance to those dealing with career struggles similar to mine. So often, we wake up and force ourselves to go to a job that offers us little in terms of satisfaction. I know I did. Sierra shows us not only how to get out of that situation but how to recognize we might be in that situation in the first place.

ACKNOWLEDGEMENTS

My gratitude and thanks go out to many people. While I may be listed as the author of this book, it takes a village to actually get it out the door!

To my husband David, who put up with late nights and my distracted conversations. You support me in my every endeavor, and I love you for letting me be me. You are a one in a million.

To my parents – Mom, you helped me become who I am today. I only wish Dad were still alive to see this book published. You both always encouraged me in everything I did and gave me a strong sense of possibility.

To my extended family – Tracy, Josh, Nicky, Mariah, Dustin, Crystal, Jamie, Jessie, and all of my aunt, uncles, and cousins. I hope you all have the chance to make your own LEAP and have the perfect careers for each of you.

To Crystle and Dorothy – you helped me to know that I could write this book. Thank you!

To the entire group of the Matrixx May 2010 – It was at that event that I finally acknowledged that I wanted to write this book. Your encouragement allowed me to get over my own fears, to get to help others overcome their fears.

To the team at Bound Publishing – you guys rock!! I came to you with only a glimmer of an idea and you helped me to turn it into a complete book. I couldn't have done it without your support and encouragement.

INTRODUCTION

*As you climb the ladder of success, be sure it's
leaning against the right building.*

**– Quoted in P.S. I Love You,
compiled by H. Jackson Brown, Jr.**

I always knew I would climb the ladder of success. I just never knew what the right ladder was. I never knew what I wanted to be when I grew up. My earliest thought was that I would grow up to be an auto mechanic, followed over the years by forest ranger, psychologist, dietician, electrical engineer, nun, medieval history professor, and computer programmer. It was that last choice that did me in.

I got a good job. It paid really well, and I liked it. My coworkers were great, and the pay was really good. I got comfortable. Did I mention that I got paid, too?

It's easy to get trapped by a well paying job, particularly if you aren't really sure what else you want to be doing. Today's society seems to revolve around money - who has it and how much. That makes it all too easy to become wed to a job that isn't the best fit for you because it pays well. You can buy things that seem to make you happy - a great house, great car, the best food and clothes. But you are still spending eight or more hours a day doing something you don't love.

I've gotten two different wake up calls, both of which I ignored. The first time I was laid off was in 1999, and I was on vacation. The company wasn't doing well; although there had been no hint at all that a layoff was coming. I was on vacation during the Thanksgiving holiday, visiting family. I got a phone call from my manager who told me I'd been laid off. I could make an appointment to come in the office and collect my personal belongings, but the layoff was effective immediately. It was only four weeks until Christmas. I was devastated. This had been my first well-paid job, and it was gone. Although I hadn't been happy in the job, instead of feeling the freedom to decide on my next career move, I felt panic. I **had** to get another job. I focused on getting another job to replace the one I'd been laid off from. Within two weeks I had a job offer which I immediately accepted.

My next position was even better pay, and it was at a very prestigious company. I felt lucky to have gotten employed there. I started working 50 to 60 hours a week. My coworkers were great people and I was paid very well. That company also offered stock options. They were jokingly referred to as "The Golden Handcuffs" because if you left the company, you lost the options. I worked at the company for nearly seven years. Then I was laid off again, and again I missed an opportunity to figure out what really made me happy.

When I was laid off the second time, I had the option of either trying to find another job within the company or taking an immediate buyout package. I was looking for guidance anywhere I could find it. I couldn't figure out what to do. I felt very secure working for the company, despite the fact that I had been laid off, and I was afraid to leave. I went back and forth. Both options had about the same monetary value, so that was no help. The weekend after I was laid off, I went on a weekend vacation with my thoughts continuing to swirl around what step I should take.

Ironically, guidance came in a gift shop. I was looking at magnets with inspirational messages on them, and saw the quote "Leap and the net will appear" by John Burroughs. It hit me hard. I immediately decided to leave the company and take my chances. Within three weeks, despite a bad economy and high unemployment rate, I had secured a new job at a great company at a higher rate of pay and with better benefits. Despite having left the security of my former employer, I had still overlooked the opportunity to assess whether my career path was the right one for me. Sure, I was climbing the ladder of success, but was I climbing the right ladder?

This probably sounds somewhat familiar. Most people, when they lose their job, immediately look for another position just like their last one. It's what we're trained to do; it's our comfort zone and skill set. As people climb the ladder of success, most never pause to figure out if it's the right ladder. They simply look for the next rung up and keep climbing. Even if they hate their job, even if they dread waking up each day knowing that they have to go back to work, they still return to that same job.

Since that time in the gift shop, "Leap and the net will appear" has continued to echo in my mind on a regular basis. Despite the good salary, I came to realize that my job wasn't the "leap" I was supposed to take. I needed to really evaluate what I wanted to do with my life. I had drifted into computer work because I enjoyed the challenge and earned good money, but computer programming was never a passion of mine. I had never discovered what I really wanted to do. I kept asking myself, "What if there is another way? What if I could look forward to waking up each day, eager to go to work?"

I began to realize that my passions lay in mobile technology. I love gadgets, tablets, mobile phones – the whole range of mobile computing technology. My happiest times have come from evangelizing the use of mobile technology and showing how that technology can have a positive impact on people's lives. I began to look around. After I made the positive commitment to myself to move into a career focused on mobile computing, doors began to open. I spent spare time blogging about mobile technology, and then finally, I changed roles and began to work on marketing of new mobile technology. The quote "Leap and the net will appear" continued to echo in my mind even as I found myself working in a role that I found very satisfying.

One Saturday morning, I woke up far earlier than usual. As I lay dozing, my mind wandered to that well-known quote, and I suddenly thought, "LEAP is an acronym. LEAP means: LEARN, ENVISION, ACT, POSSESS. You should write a book about that." I got out of bed immediately and started writing. I finally knew exactly what I was supposed to do. I knew that my success in finding my career path could help others find their perfect career.

DOROTHY'S STORY

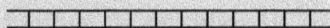

Dorothy was a recruiting officer, helping her company find and hire new college graduates. Like many of us, she went to work each day, did her job to the best of her ability, and came home, worn out and tired. She liked her coworkers and found some parts of her job enjoyable, but overall, she knew it wasn't the right job for her. She had been doing the same thing for over ten years, and she wasn't sure what else to do. She knew and understood her job, knew what to do, knew the systems and the rules. She knew how to be successful. Making a change would be hard. She needed the steady paycheck as she raised her two kids.

One day, as a way to treat herself after an especially stressful week, Dorothy had a facial. Unfortunately, the esthetician who gave her the facial was not good at her job. The facial was a failure, but it gave Dorothy an idea. She knew that she could give a far better facial than the one she had just received. An idea was born. Dorothy wanted to become an esthetician.

As you read Dorothy's story throughout this book, you will see how Dorothy went through the four LEAP steps and now has her own perfect career. She LEARNed what she wanted, ENVISIONed herself doing the job, ACTed on a daily basis, and she now POSSESSes a career as an esthetician. She loves to get up each day, knowing that she gets to make people feel better and more relaxed through her services.

CHAPTER 1:

CLIMBING THE RIGHT LADDER USING LEAP

Your time is limited, so don't waste it living someone else's life. Don't be trapped by dogma - which is living with the results of other people's thinking. Don't let the noise of other's opinions drown out your own inner voice. And most important, have the courage to follow your heart and intuition. They somehow already know what you truly want to become. Everything else is secondary.

– Steve Jobs

1

Are you climbing the *right* ladder to success? Climbing the right ladder feels good. You are happy with your career and you look forward to going to work. You feel yourself progressively improving your career options and can see a bright future for yourself.

Unfortunately, people are increasingly climbing the wrong ladder, which leads to job dissatisfaction and unhappiness. Over 55% of Americans are dissatisfied with their jobs, according to a study in January 2010 by The Conference Board. That is the lowest level of job satisfaction in 20 years. When you add in the nearly 10% of people who are currently unemployed, you get nearly two out of every three people who are climbing the wrong ladder.

The reasons vary for such a high rate of job dissatisfaction – organization health, job design, management quality, and pay. "Survivor syndrome" also played a role, where people, left employed after layoffs, must do additional work for the same pay, leading to longer hours and more stress.

All of these reasons assume that the employee likes their line of work. It doesn't matter how great your work environment is if you hate the kind of work you do. You have to enjoy doing the daily tasks to have a good chance of being satisfied with your career. One of my early jobs was working as a bookstore sales clerk. I thought I would like the job – I love books, the bookstore was a favorite of mine, and my coworkers were great people.

Unfortunately, I disliked working retail. I wanted more challenge from my daily work, and I wasn't getting it at the bookstore. The line of work wasn't the right choice for me, and I was dissatisfied in my job, despite its appealing characteristics.

Are you satisfied with your current career? Sometimes people are unaware of underlying job dissatisfaction, so here are some questions to help you out.

1. Does job stress affect your health? Do you have high blood pressure, ulcers, or other health issues that relate to your job stress?

2. How often do you dread going to work? There are days when everyone would rather stay home, but if you dread going to work more often than not, then the cause may be deeper than simply wanting to stay in bed.

3. How long does it take for you to decompress after work? Most people need a few minutes, but if it takes hours or affects you ability to relate to your family or friends, then you may have a larger problem.

4. Do you require "help" to decompress? This help could take many forms, including food, drink, watching TV, or playing video games. While none

of these are in themselves problematic, they can become a problem if they keep you from enjoying your free time. If you find yourself regularly using "self-medication" to soothe your emotional stress, then you may not like your job.

5. Do you waste time to keep from doing your job? If you don't like what you're doing, it's easy to procrastinate to avoid doing unpleasant tasks. Again, a certain amount of procrastination is normal, but if you find yourself spending significant time each day doing something other than what you are paid to do, you have a problem.

6. Do you spend money on unnecessary treats you think you deserve because you have worked hard? Whenever I felt like I was working too hard or I felt stressed at work, "Retail Therapy" came to the rescue, usually in the form of a nice new handbag or dress. It doesn't matter whether your treats are shoes or snow globes, if you buy them merely for the short-lived thrill, you may be masking a deeper dissatisfaction.

7. Do you wake up each day eager to go to work? Do you feel like you are making a difference in your own and others' lives? If you won the lottery today, would you continue to work in your current job? If not, what would you do instead?

You may have identified with a number of the characteristics of job dissatisfaction, but you still think you like your job. It may surprise you to realize that you don't like your job. I know it was a surprise to me at one point. I worked at a high-tech company. The hours were long, but I loved my coworkers and I enjoyed teaching people about new computer technology. However, the company needed to downsize and my job was eliminated. I was very upset because I identified much of my own sense of self-worth with that job. I thought I was very satisfied.

However, once I left the company and spent some time away from the tense atmosphere, I realized how stressed I had been in the job. While there had certainly been elements that I had enjoyed, overall, the job had not been good for me. My health was affected, it took hours for me to decompress after work, and I spent a significant portion of my disposable income on "Retail Therapy." Sometimes what seems like a great job in the beginning can turn into the wrong one over time. Recognizing the change, however, can be very difficult.

RECOGNIZING TOXIC ENVIRONMENTS

People who are in jobs that are going bad don't always recognize how toxic the environment is until they leave. If you put a frog in boiling water, the frog will immediately jump out. Similarly, if you take on a new job that is not right for you, you will likely realize it and leave quickly. However, if you put a frog in cool water and then heat the water up to boiling, the frog won't recognize the increasing temperature and know to jump out.

This story is a constant reminder to me to assess whether I'm being "boiled alive" – allowing myself to remain in a harmful environment. What may have started as a great place to work may no longer be ideal due to changes in the environment or changes in your own needs.

On the other hand, you may be doing the wrong job even if your current environment is tempting. Think back to how you got into your current line of work. Many people spend more time choosing their wardrobes than they do choosing their careers! I suspect a lot of people fell into their current line of work, much like I fell into working in high tech. Whether you consciously chose your profession or not, it may not be the perfect career for you.

REASONS PEOPLE STAY

At first glance it may seem that the reasons people become dissatisfied with their careers vary significantly. However, my years of research have shown that the problem really boils down to two things:

1. Uncertainty - not really knowing what else to do.

2. Fear – of failure, success, salary impact, or other indefinable fears.

In this book, we will address the questions of knowing what to do and overcoming the fears preventing your from changing careers. Through the exercises in each chapter, we will work through questions and issues that may have prevented you from transitioning to a new career in the past. You will get the opportunity to learn more about yourself, your motivations, and what type of work will make you the most satisfied with your career.

We only get one chance at life, and we never know when the time is up. It wouldn't necessarily be a problem to spend five to ten years doing a job we disliked if we got to live forever. I won't live forever, and I want to make the most of the time I know I have. I know you do too. We have the choice. We can spend that time in jobs we hate, or we can choose to get the careers we want.

How do you want to spend your time?

INTRODUCTION TO THE LEAP SYSTEM

As I went through the process of finding my own perfect career, I developed a four-step system called LEAP, an acronym that stands for:

LEARN

ENVISION

ACT

POSSESS

The first step is to LEARN – learn what you want in your career and understand what has prevented you from achieving it in the past. This is frequently the hardest part, but I have exercises that will help you to clarify your perfect career.

Once your perfect career is clear, you can actively ENVISION yourself working in that new field, taking advantage of techniques used by astronauts and Olympic athletes.

It is when you ACT towards achieving that goal that you will begin to experience real joy, as the seemingly impossible becomes reality, step by step.

Finally, you POSSESS the career you have dreamed of. However, it is likely at this point that you will have created even bigger career goals for yourself and want to go back to the beginning and LEAP again!

In the following chapters, we will walk through each step of the LEAP system. Take the time to understand each step and go through the exercises. You won't get your prefect career just by reading this book. You will have to do the work along the way to make sure you know where and how you are making the transition. However, if you follow the system and put the effort into the exercises, you will have a path to take you where you want to go.

CRYSTLE'S STORY

Crystle had worked in a variety of jobs trying to find a good fit. She worked for many years as an administrative assistant in a technology company but she knew that her lack of a college degree was holding her back. She went to night school and got her bachelor's degree but, like many college students, she still didn't know what she wanted to do with the degree. She found a job as a program manager, which seemed ideal for someone who was really good at keeping people organized.

Even as Crystle climbed the ladder of success, she kept wondering if she was doing the right thing. Her heart and passion were certainly not in technology program management. As she started going through the steps of LEAP, Crystle was initially stuck on LEARN. She didn't know what she wanted to do. With help, she finally realized that her passion lay in shoes. Crystle simply loves shoes, and that feeling is infectious. Combined with her natural flair for selling, Crystle decided that her future was in selling shoes. She is getting ready to open her new shoe business, and her future now seems full of possibilities. She's excited and eager, ready to take on the challenge.

LIMITING BELIEFS

According to author Napoleon Hill, "A goal is a dream with a deadline." In the land of dreams, it's easy to allow oneself to imagine a different future. Once you decide to pursue a dream, it becomes a goal, and that's when the problems and obstacles begin to present themselves.

As children, our parents instill in us values, morals, and a sense of right and wrong. They also instill a sense of the possible and the impossible. Children hear the statements that their parents make. "We can't afford that." "That's too expensive." "You aren't smart enough to be a doctor." "Girls can't be engineers." "Boys don't do theater." Unlike lessons on morality, these limitations are generally not consciously taught. They are, however, frequently passed down from generation to generation, which is why most families only incrementally improve their socio-economic position over each generation. These types of beliefs in the possible and impossible are Limiting Beliefs. As you accept and internalize Limiting Beliefs, you bury your ability to truly uncover the life you desire and find your perfect career. By understanding your Limiting Beliefs, you can overcome them and move towards your perfect career.

Limiting Beliefs are frequently so deeply hidden that you don't even know you have them. They cripple you in your efforts to make changes in your life because you end up sabotaging yourself. Shakespeare wrote, "Our doubts are traitors, and make us lose the good we oft might win by fearing to attempt." Self-doubt and fear frequently lead back to Limiting Beliefs. Only by understanding your Limiting Beliefs will you be able to achieve your highest success.

Despite your Limiting Beliefs, there are two pieces of good news. The first is that you can achieve anything. Yes, anything – I mean it. However, the price you have to pay to achieve some goals may be beyond what you are willing to pay. The price you pay for small goals is small, easily paid. But the price for the big goals requires commitment and dedication, which is generally only "worth it" for something you want desperately. Few people would go through the long years and expense of medical school if they didn't have a real desire to be a doctor. Conversely, it's far easier to work in fast food, but the rewards are far less as well.

The second piece of good news is that you don't have to conquer all of your Limiting Beliefs at one time, nor do you have to completely conquer them to begin pursuing your perfect career. For many people, completely overcoming their Limiting Beliefs happens at the same time as achieving success. At that point, their Limiting Beliefs simply fade away.

EXERCISE:

Think back to your childhood. What Limiting Beliefs did you learn from your parents? Write your answers to the questions below:

1. What were your parents' opinions of wealthy people? Positive? Negative?

2. What did your parents say when you told them your childhood dreams of what you wanted to be when you grew up?

3. Did your parents or teachers encourage you to daydream?

4. Were you supported in your efforts when you were in school, or were you discouraged from trying harder? Did people tell you that you were smart or did they say you were average? Did you believe them?

5. Did your parents succeed in their life? Did they complain about missed dreams or missed opportunities?

6. Did your parents have a scarcity mentality? Did they feel that there was only a little to go around, so you'd better grab what you could get?

Now that you understand some of your Limiting Beliefs, you have to decide consciously which of those beliefs you agree with and which you want to reject. Choose carefully – those beliefs will shape your future. Do not accept limitations that prevent you from achieving your dreams. If your parents believed that only crooked people became wealthy, then that belief can be a barrier to your own wealth.

As you go back through your list of answers, think about your responses and whether that belief works with you or against you. Any answers that reveal beliefs of lack, limitation, or restriction are probably not helping you achieve your goals. Answers that are open, inclusive, and show an understanding of the abundance in nature will allow you to quickly have your perfect career.

Review the negative answers and turn the negative answers into their positive counterpart. If you believe that you can't be a lawyer because you're not smart enough, change that into a belief that you are fully capable of doing anything you want to do. At first, you will probably not believe the statements that you write. But you are trying to overwrite years of negative programming, so keep reading and saying the positive statements whenever you find yourself drifting back to your Limiting Belief.

As you continually fight back against the Limiting Beliefs with positive statements, the Limiting Beliefs will begin to lose their power over you. You'll begin to find yourself thinking the positive thoughts more frequently as your subconscious accepts these truths.

CHAPTER 2:

LEARN WHAT YOU WANT

*So let your deepest desires direct your aim.
Set your sights far above the 'reasonable'
target. The power of purpose is profound
only if you have a desire that stirs the heart.*

— Price Pritchett

2

What kind of career do you really want? For many people, this is a very hard question to answer. A good place to start is to think about what you wanted to be "when you grew up." As a child, we frequently are in better touch with our real desires and our real talents. The Rev. Michael Beckwith tells a story from his childhood. He had been nominated to be the class treasurer; this required him to give a speech to the assembled school. He was very afraid to do the speech and tried to get out of it. However, he was compelled to speak. Much to his surprise, once in front of the group, he spoke eloquently and all fear of speaking dropped away. That talent that he discovered as a child was forgotten for years, but it resurfaced immediately when he learned his calling to speak to people spiritually. Now, he makes his living as the spiritual director of Agape International and speaks to groups on a daily basis.

After years of childhood conditioning as to what is possible and impossible, most people give up completely on their "impossible" dreams. But dreams can come true well into adulthood just as they can in youth. Both Thomas Edison and Albert Einstein were considered unintelligent dreamers as children, dreaming impossible dreams. Both men had first careers that they later set aside when they began to focus on what were truly their perfect careers. Edison's inventing ability was hampered by his job as a telegraph operator, but the training that he received in that job helped him to design a number of important inventions, including the stock ticker. Similarly, Einstein briefly held a job as a patent office clerk, which gave him insights into what ultimately became his theories on space and time.

In both Edison's and Einstein's cases, they did not let their early jobs keep them from ultimately achieving success in their perfect careers. They knew what they wanted to do with their lives. Despite training and a "good job", they both had dreams and goals that were larger than their current positions. In both cases, they outgrew their original careers.

While your career may have been right for you at a previous point in your life, it may not be as good a fit anymore. Or perhaps you didn't know what you wanted to do and drifted into a job path that paid the bills and gave you time to enjoy your social life. Regardless of where you have been, now is the time to choose where you are going.

For many people, the process of discovering what they want from a career is surprisingly complex. While we all seem to know people who knew from an early age what they were meant to do in life, for most of us, there was never a clear answer.

I started off at an early age wanting to be an auto mechanic, which moved into building things, then psychology, novel writing, and professional reading. That brings me to age 12. During my teens, I didn't have any firm idea of what I wanted to do professionally. As I went off to college, the college president told my parents that the average college student switches majors five times. Never one to be average, I switched majors six times in four years, working my way through such diverse majors as electrical engineering, medieval studies, religious studies, and technical writing, before settling into computer science and mathematics. Yet I still didn't know what my right ladder was. It took several years and many false starts before I started to know myself well enough to know what I wanted out of life.

The fact is that most people focus on external factors when choosing a career. They think about the money, the prestige, or possibly, the impact on society. Well-meaning family, friends, or school counselors frequently try to influence them. But focusing on these external trappings often doesn't lead to career satisfaction. You have to look inside to get the real story.

The most important aspects to job happiness are the characteristics of the job. What will you actually be doing day-in and day-out if you have that career? While salary and social impact are important factors, if you faint at the sight of blood, you shouldn't try to be a surgeon. It may seem simple, and it **is** simple, but too often we overlook the obvious. Unless you like what you are actually going to be doing everyday, you won't like your job. It doesn't matter how great the company is or how much you love your coworkers, if you don't like your daily tasks, then you need a different career.

I've created a series of exercises to help guide your thought process as you search for the job characteristics that are most important to you. One important thing to know is that there are no right or wrong answers here. Answer these questions with the first thoughts that come to your mind.

EXERCISE: PERFECT CAREER CHARACTERISTICS

1. How much interaction with other people or coworkers do you want each day? For some people, working alone is ideal. For others, significant interaction with others is a necessary part of their career.

2. How long are you willing to commute each day? Do you want to drive, ride public transit, walk, or ride a bicycle to work? I once was offered a job at an excellent company, working with interesting people on a great project. However, I would have been spending two hours or more each day commuting. I declined that offer due to the long commute.

3. What hours do you want to work? Consider both the number of hours and time of day you find perfect. If you hate mornings, then a job where you have to be at work by 7:00 am will not be a great fit for you. If you want a part-time job, then full-time work isn't an option. I prefer to start work at about 9:00 am. My brain seems to be working best around that time.

I had a job once where I had to be at work by 7:15 am. While I was physically present, I wasn't mentally "all there" until around 9:00. It's best to accept that fact and find a job that allows you to work your best hours.

4. Where do you want to work? What is your ideal work environment? For some, working at home is perfect. For others, a busy office environment works best. Personally, I like working at the coffee shop. There is a small buzz of activity, but no one wants to talk to me, so I have a certain amount of privacy while still in public. Think about times when you have been the most productive and happiest. What kind of work environment was that?

5. Do you like what you do each day? Sometimes people have a tendency to romanticize certain occupations, only to discover later that the day-to-day reality isn't what they want. You may think that being a doctor means helping people every day, but it also means a lot of paperwork, scheduling headaches, and dealing with unhappy and unhealthy people. That may not be what you expected. You could discover that your perfect career isn't what you thought it was.

6. What do you NOT want? Many times it is easier to determine what we want to exclude from our lives than what we want to include. As you think about each thing you do not want, think about how to turn it into a positive statement. The positive statement is what you need to focus on.

What you do not want	Positive Statement
I do not want to work every day and I don't want to be awakened by an alarm clock.	I want the freedom to choose my working hours.
I do not want to spend time with negative people.	I want happy, fulfilling relationships with positive, up-beat people.
I do not want to spend my whole day on the telephone.	I want to work with people face-to-face.

7. What did you dream of doing or being when you were a child? Would you still want that dream? Does it inspire you to a new dream?

8. What do you like to do best? What brings you the most joy when you are doing it? It could be something you currently do professionally or it could be a hobby or other interest. It may be a small element of your current career – maybe you enjoy working with the public but you don't like working in retail.

9. Do you want to turn your hobby into a career? Don't feel limited because "there's no way to make money doing that." Maybe you love photography and would like to be a professional photographer, but you've been told "No one can do that for a job." If you love to do it, list it. Is there anyone, anywhere, living a rich and fulfilled life doing what you love? Then you can too!

Take time to think through and write out your answers for each of the exercises. It is only by taking the time to LEARN what you want that you will be able to achieve the career of your dreams.

It's possible that even after these exercises you won't have a firm career goal. That's okay. You should still have a much clearer understanding of the characteristics that you want for your perfect career. Start researching careers that involve the most important characteristics. The Internet can be very helpful in finding career descriptions that you can match to your defined characteristics. Even if you don't have a name for what you want to do, you probably have a pretty good idea of what you'll do each day. Then, when the perfect career appears, you be able to recognize it and make the LEAP.

DOROTHY'S STORY

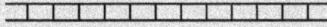

When Dorothy had the bad facial, she knew she could do better. She decided to LEARN more about what it would take to become an esthetician.

Dorothy read about the necessary training and certifications. She learned about the local schools that train estheticians and found out which schools were better than others. Everything she learned made her more and more convinced that this was the right path for her. As she learned more about the daily activities of an esthetician and the range of services that most estheticians provide, she determined that those daily activities were something she would enjoy. She compared her list of career characteristics against those required to be an esthetician and decided that it was a perfect fit.

TYPES OF GOALS

While learning what your perfect career should be is an important first step, there is another skill that is equally important to LEAP to your perfect career. You need to be able to set and achieve goals. If you did your exercises well, you did not limit yourself to "reasonable" options when you were learning about your perfect career. That may mean you came out of the exercises with a perfect career that you either don't know how to achieve, or you don't know how to make money doing it. That is fine; once you understand the basic types of goals and how to use goal-setting to guide your progress, the method to achieve your perfect career will become clearer to you.

There are three basic types of goals:

TYPE 1: REALISTIC.

Realistic goals are goals that you understand how to accomplish. Most people never get beyond setting realistic goals because their low self-confidence keeps them from believing they can do more. These "goals" are well within a person's comfort zone. For careers, realistic goals include doing the same type of jobs as your parents or relatives. You know exactly what is required of you to do that type of work.

Examples: taking over the family business, becoming a teacher like your parents, working at McDonald's as your first job.

I had a friend in high school. While Jackie was very intelligent, she didn't believe she could go to college. No one in her family had gone to college, so it wasn't something within her comfort zone. Her mother worked in a factory job, and Jackie figured she would probably do the same thing. She didn't dare to dream of more.

TYPE 2. STRETCH GOALS.

If you know how to get from your current state to your goal, but doing so gives you a bit of fear, you are probably thinking about a stretch goal. Stretch goals go beyond what you have done in the past, but they push a little bit at the edges of your Limiting Beliefs. For people who are actively trying to improve their lives, stretch goals are the most common. A person can set a clear path to the goal and set interim, smaller goals along the way. While stretch goals feel - and are - difficult, they still feel only a little outside a person's comfort zone.

When you set a stretch goal for a career, it typically involves setting a goal for a job a few steps above any previous success you may have had. As a child, that means dreaming of a career that will earn more respect or money than the careers of your parents. Most parents want their children to have more in life than they did; therefore many parents push their children into careers that will have better economic and social positions.

Examples: asking for a promotion at work (especially if you've been doing higher level work already), making the transition from individual contributor to manager, applying your existing skills in a new field

Although Jackie thought she would probably end up in the same factory job as her mother, there was a part of her that wanted more from her life. In our senior year of high school, when I began looking at possible colleges, I took Jackie with me on college visits. I talked to her frequently about the student loans, grants, and scholarships that I learned about so that she could see a way to pay for college. During the course of our senior year, Jackie began applying to colleges and applying for financial aid. She had set the stretch goal of attending college. She graduated and loves her career as a teacher.

TYPE 3. FANTASY.

Truly exciting changes occur in your life when you can embrace your fantasies. These are the dreams you have no idea how to achieve. Most people, because they have no idea how to achieve these fantasy goals, don't even try. However, when you commit yourself to a fantasy goal, strange and amazing things start to happen. People who can help you show up in your life. Money necessary for your goal will appear. Opportunities will appear and doors will open in unexpected ways. Once you begin to embrace your fantasy goals, then synchronicity begins to step in and cause you to act.

Career fantasies can be quite varied. For one person, the fantasy is to quit a very highly-paid, stressful career to focus on his love of flowers and start a flower shop. Another may dream of becoming the CEO of a large corporation, even though she isn't even on the management team. For most fantasy jobs, you have no idea how to move from your current position to the fantasy. Consequently you don't make any move at all. However, the most joy and career satisfaction typically comes from achieving your Fantasy career.

Examples: become a successful actor, be president of a Fortune 500 company, own your own business.

I once had a coworker who was a very successful manager at a technology company. His day-to-day job was stressful, but he performed it very well. He spent most of the day solving problems, in meetings with other managers and answering email.

However, he dreamed of owning a hardware store. He would talk about the hardware store and types of products it would sell, where he would locate it, and how much joy he would get from owning his own business. But for that person, the hardware store was a fantasy that would never happen. He had no idea how to go from managing a team of computer programmers to owning a hardware store. It was far outside his set of Limiting Beliefs.

Now that you know the types of goals, you need to start focusing on the Type 3 Fantasy Goals. Your mind is a strange and complex thing, and the universe is even more strange and complex. When you focus on small goals, you get small results, assuming you get any results at all. If you allow yourself to focus on BIG goals, scary, Type 3 Fantasy Goals, then strange things happen. Your mind starts shifting, opportunities appear, and the previously "impossible" becomes possible. Research has shown that we are more committed to bigger goals, those goals that require us to focus more of our thought and attention. By focusing on your Fantasy Goal, you will become more and more committed to it, and increase your chances of success.

Now that you have a clear idea of your perfect career and you know more about goal setting, it's important to begin putting goals in place to achieve your perfect career.

CREATE YOUR CAREER STATEMENT

Review the career characteristics you created earlier in this chapter. Now take those career characteristics and provide even more detail. Describe your perfect career with as much detail as you can. Include details like:

Where do you work – the size of the company, your office type, the environment in which you spend most of your time

- What are your coworkers like? Or, do you work alone?

- How many hours per week do you work?

- What do you enjoy the most about this perfect career?

- How much do you want to get paid?

This description should be as long as it takes for you to fully describe your perfect career. It may be several pages long if you know enough detail about your perfect career.

Now, take that description and condense it to one or two sentences. This should be the essence of the long description, meaningful to you and still descriptive to others. The description should be in the form of an affirmation, like it has already happened to you. This is your Career Statement. The idea is to condense your excitement about your perfect career into a very brief statement that you can repeat to yourself several times per day.

Examples of Career Statements could be:

- I am a successful chef. My restaurant is the talk of the town and everyone wants to eat there.

- I am a thriving personal trainer with a full appointment schedule of clients. My clients refer their friends and family to me because they are pleased with their progress."

- I am a highly successful business consultant, working with Fortune 100 companies to improve processes and identify waste. I work when I want, for whom I want.

- I am a bestselling author and keynote speaker. My books have improved the lives of people around the world.

Some of you may have set a very large, ambitious Career Statement. If so, you may want to break down that goal into phases. Each phase should have ACTions you can take and a specific end point when you know you POSSESS the outcome you are seeking. Your LEAP plan allows you the flexibility to set large or small career goals. Simply by treating each phase as a separate LEAP, you can go through several smaller LEAPs to achieve a giant LEAP. The key element to creating phases is making sure that you know the definition of "done." If you can define successful completion of any step along the path to your ultimate perfect career, then that step qualifies as its own LEAP phase. If you can't ENVISION what success would be for that step, then you probably are taking too small of a step. Try to encompass more steps towards your Career Statement and you will find that balance point where your step is worthwhile in itself, yet also a step along the way towards an even larger goal.

It is easy to stay motivated when you see progress each day. Celebrate each and every milestone phase toward your ultimate career goal and you can see how far you have come in your journey.

EXERCISE:

Write your Career Statement on a small card and read it at least twice daily. By keeping your new career in the front of your mind, you allow your subconscious to work on ways to achieve that goal, even when you aren't thinking about it directly.

Once a week, read your long description of your perfect career. Make adjustments if necessary, as you move along the path. Keep the entire goal in mind.

CRYSTLE'S STORY

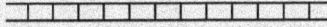

Crystle always knew she loved shoes. It was practically a running joke among her family and friends. But she didn't believe that she could turn that passion into a career. Her Limiting Beliefs told her that she was too old and she didn't know how to run a business. Through exercises to reprogram her Limiting Beliefs, Crystle was able to set the goal to start her own shoe business. She began to learn more about the characteristics she wanted to have in her shoe business and how she wanted to be involved. She decided that she wanted to be able to select the shoe styles so a franchise operation wasn't going to fit her requirements. She would have to open an independent business. She continued to learn more about what it would take to open a small business and overcame the mental objections that her Limiting Beliefs tried to raise. She knew she could do it and she felt the inspiration of setting a true Fantasy Goal.

CHAPTER 3:

ENVISION YOUR PERFECT CAREER

*The soul is dyed the color of its thoughts.
Think only on those things that are in line
with your principles and can bear the full
light of day. The content of your character is
your choice. Day by day, what you choose,
what you think, and what you do is who you
become. Your integrity is your destiny....
it is the light that guides your way.*

– Heraclitus

3

You know the right ladder for you, but there's a part of you that is probably uncertain because you have no idea how to bring it into reality. That's natural. You have been working by a set of rules your entire life and I'm asking you to change that rulebook. Now we're going to step back from that scary place and do something that should be completely enjoyable.

We're going back to your childhood – sitting still and imagining.

When I was a child, I had a very active imagination. I could easily imagine a purple sky with fluffy red clouds and yellow trees bathed in light from the green sun. There weren't many children in my neighborhood when I was very small, so I spent a lot of time alone, imagining a complete made-up world filled with friends. I didn't know that developing my vivid imagination was going to be so helpful later.

Even if you did not spend lazy hours imagining strange new worlds when you were a child, you still have the ability to ENVISION.

ENVISION is just a fancy term for daydreaming, but with focus, direction, and goals. When you envision, you pick the specific future you want and, letting your imagination take flight, envision all of the details. In the previous chapter, you wrote a detailed description of your perfect career. You can use that description as a starting point as you begin to ENVISION.

The key to successful envisioning is filling in the details – imagining the entire reality and feeling the joy. Without the joy, you've merely painted a pretty mental image. You have to infuse the vision with every ounce of joy, happiness, desire and longing you have. The emotional connection you have to that dream is what gives it power and what gives you the strength and the focus to keep your dream alive. Without the emotion, you might as well be watching TV and eating chips, because, although you have just seen a good show, it wasn't your future. In order for it to become your future, you have to feel it, want it, and see it.

ENVISIONING IN ATHLETICS

Envisioning may seem like a strange thing to consider in a book about reaching your perfect career. But performance researchers (who call it 'envisioning' and not 'imagining') know that being able to envision success is vital to achieving success. When NASA was training the first astronauts, no one knew exactly what they would have to face in space and during the lunar landing. But to the extent possible, the scientists at NASA had the astronauts envision each step of the process until "memories" of the future events were deeply engrained in the astronauts' minds.

Similarly, elite athletes are trained to envision their performance. Researchers have even hooked up sophisticated equipment to the athlete's bodies both while they were working out and while they were merely envisioning themselves performing their sports. While the athletes were envisioning their performance, the same mental activity was recorded and the same muscles fired like they would during the real event. The brain was rehearsing the actual contest without the body performing it. Additional studies have shown that the performance increase from envisioning is comparable to the performance increase from increased physical training.

In 1984, Mary Lou Retton was a 16-year-old athlete waiting to perform her final gymnastics routine at the Olympic Games in Los Angeles. Although she was a world champion performer, six weeks prior to the Olympics, she suffered a knee injury that required surgery. Although the knee had healed, the surgery had affected her ability to practice those last few weeks before the Games.

"In the weeks before the Olympics, Mary Lou often lay in her bed with her eyes closed and let her imagination romp. She would visualize herself on each piece of equipment, performing her best routines and hitting every move perfectly." (Footnote the source: Sullivan, George. Mary Lou Retton. New York:Julian Messner, 1985) During her first performances at the Games, Retton performed well and she was in third place going into the final day of competition. Retton had previously spent hours rehearsing her routine and, as she lay in bed the night before her final performance, she envisioned the routine again and again in her mind.

Going into the last event, she was slightly behind Ekaterina Szabo, the Romanian star. Szabo, an excellent athlete, scored a 9.90 out of 10 in her final routine. For Retton to win, she would need a perfect 10 on the vault. Anything less would mean second place.

Retton ran down the runway to the vault, hit the springboard and went 14 feet into the air, doing a back somersault and double twist. She landed with both feet planted. Perfect 10!

Olympic rules state that competitors must do the vault event two times. So after her first perfect 10, Retton stepped right back on the runway and repeated her flawless performance. The envisioning had worked. Despite her injury, despite the surgery, Mary Lou Retton won the gold medal.

You harness that same power every time you envision the career of your dreams!

However, like any skill, envisioning takes practice. It is likely that the first time you try to envision your perfect career you will be a little vague on the details. You may not be a person who spent much time dreaming as a child, so it may not come naturally. Don't worry. One of the beauties of practicing this skill is that you get better at it with practice. Over time, you will be able to see more and more detail. You will find that with each session you add more detail and the vision becomes more complete.

TECHNIQUES TO IMPROVE ENVISIONING

Another technique that improves your ability to envision is to add movement. Think of the difference between a photograph and a movie. While both can be detailed and evoke an emotional response, the movie will likely have a stronger response than the still photo. Similarly, an active vision will have a stronger impact than a static vision. It is much easier to ENVISION something that is active. Think about the interior of your car. While you can probably pull up a pretty good picture of it, the picture probably becomes clearer if you imagine driving the car, your hands wrapped around the steering wheel, putting the car into gear, adjusting the mirrors. Imagining the motion involves pulling in different parts of your brain, which improves your ability to visualize.

As you are viewing the image in your mind's eye, note your viewpoint. Frequently when I am forming a new vision, I discover that I am viewing the scene as a third party. I may even see myself like an actor performing a role in the scene. When I change my point of view to that of a participant rather than an observer, I get a far stronger emotional connection to the goal. It is the emotional response that gives power to the vision. Your mind gives more thought and more commitment to a goal that you are emotionally connected to.

As you begin to envision your perfect career, you may discover you don't know some of the details about the work you will do. Learn as much as you can about the career you want so that you can accurately envision yourself performing well in it. Interview people who have the same or a similar position. Most people are willing to give a few minutes of their time to do an informational interview about their position.

It is vitally important that you become 100% committed to having your perfect career. It is very easy to have lingering doubts about whether you will be able to transition to it. As these doubts and negative thoughts surface, acknowledge them and learn from them. Your doubts and negative thoughts help you to recognize which Limiting Beliefs are keeping you from moving forward. Once you understand and overcome them, bring your full vision back to the front of your mind and feel the joy of possessing your ideal career. The most powerful antidote for fear is happiness.

When doubts creep into my mind, I try to discover their roots – where they come from. Most often, they spring from fear. It could be fear of failure or even fear of success. People fear success far more often than you might think, because success means change. When you succeed in having your perfect career, your life will change, taking you outside your current comfort zone. This can cause definite feelings of discomfort and unease, despite having achieved your goal.

OVERCOMING FEAR

Personal development expert Bob Proctor refers to these uncomfortable feelings as your Terror Barrier, and other personal growth leaders have their own names for this difficult chasm. As you approach or even envision achieving something far beyond your current situation, you usually encounter the Terror Barrier, where your mind starts creating seemingly insurmountable obstacles to achieving your goal.

Know this – there are no insurmountable obstacles. If you can commit to your vision 100 percent and keep that vision before you, you can achieve it. The obstacles will either melt away, change or you will discover a way around them – **if** you keep to your commitment and keep your vision strong.

DOROTHY'S STORY

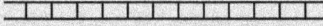

For quite a while, various fears had kept Dorothy from pursuing a career as an esthetician. She needed a steady income to cover household expenses and to provide for her children. However, as the dream grew within her, she committed herself completely. Dorothy knew the importance of envisioning herself as an esthetician. She spent time learning about the daily activities of an esthetician. Then she let herself dream about having that career. She envisioned having her own room with a proper chair for clients to relax in. She imagined the hot towels, the lotions, serene music filling the room. She imagined herself giving a facial to a client and exactly what it would be like. As she envisioned this future, she felt peace and joy. She knew that this was an appropriate path for her. She knew she had found her perfect career. As she made her commitment to transition to that new career, the fears and obstacles started to disappear. She found a way to pay for the necessary schooling while still paying her other expenses.

Had Dorothy not committed herself 100 percent to following her dream, she could easily have been swayed as difficulties arose. But by ENVISIONing her future career, she was able to move past the obstacles and keep her focus on the final goal.

As you begin to ENVISION your perfect career, you may also get pushback from your Terror Barrier. The obstacles you raise in your mind's eye are a part of your past conditioning, a product of your Limiting Beliefs. All entrepreneurs must overcome their own Terror Barriers.

I was raised to believe that getting a good job meant you were set for life. A job was security, the path to the good life. However, as I quickly discovered, that was a myth. I was laid off from my first "good job" as the economy dropped. This forced me to re-think that limiting belief and realize that I owned my own career and needed to manage my future myself.

A common obstacle that many people face when thinking of making a major change in career path is a salary fear. A major job change may cause a temporary reduction in your income. While some see this as an insurmountable obstacle, it is important to see the change in the context of the rest of your life. When I was particularly unhappy with my job, I spent a lot of money on unnecessary purchases, most of them shoes. I didn't need the shoes, but I figured I had "earned" them because of the stress of my well-paid job. I didn't realize at the time how much of my salary was spent on emotional Band-Aids, to make me feel better since I was unfulfilled by my job. As I moved into a job that was better suited to my needs, I started spending less money on unnecessary purchases.

While income and expenses are easy to track, the stress of a bad career choice can have even larger effects, causing stress in your relationships, affecting your health, and creating a downward spiral of emotional unhappiness. Making a career change can have effects beyond your day-to-day work. It can improve other aspects of your life as you begin to allow your joy to spill into them. Imagine how much more joyful your life would be if the worry and anger you feel from your job were replaced by satisfaction and happiness of having your perfect career. Just as having the wrong job can cause a downward spiral, having the right career can create a positive upward spiral.

EXERCISE:

Set aside 15 minutes of uninterrupted time and find a comfortable space. Settle into a comfortable chair and relax. You want to associate comfortable, safe feelings with your visions of your perfect career. As you begin to relax, start to think about working in your new career.

Envision your perfect career. See through your own eyes what your life could be like once you are working each day at a job you love. Feel the joy! See the important people in your life and the role they have in the life you are envisioning. Feel the joy of the changes that having your perfect career will have on those important people – your family and friends. See how the daily rhythm of your life will change. Where and how will you spend your time? Who are you working with? If you are self-employed, where is your office? What kinds of work tools do you need to perform your new job? Will your employer provide those or do you need to make changes in your home workspace?

Experience this vision and joy at least twice per day. When you awaken in the morning, envision going to work at your perfect career, even as you go to work in your current job. Start your day reading your Career Statement and envisioning the achievement of the goal. Starting your day this way is a powerful reminder of where you are going and sets the tone for your day.

Similarly, as you go to bed at night, read your Career Statement again. Envision what your day would have been like if you already had that career. See yourself performing the daily tasks of your new career. Then, as you wake, start the positive cycle again. Each day it will become easier to envision possessing your perfect career, because each day you are one step closer to the career of your dreams.

CHAPTER 4:

ACT EVERY DAY

Doing is a quantum leap from imagining.

– Barbara Sher

4

You have LEARNed what you want and can ENVISION your future. The next step – ACT! It doesn't matter how well you envision your future if you never take any steps towards making that vision a reality. Many frustrated dreamers are caught in unhappy lives because they never take the steps necessary to make their dreams come true.

When the time comes to ACT, it doesn't matter if you have no idea what to do first. Just pick something every day and do it. When you think back on your schooling, that was probably one of your first lessons. You could never learn multiplication if you hadn't first learned addition. You could never become a doctor without years of formal training as well as practical, on-the-job learning during an internship. These small steps taken every day accumulate into major changes in a very short time.

Similarly, as you approach you career, there will likely be steps you have to take prior to being able to LEAP into that job. The steps may involve training, which could include going to school again. Even more difficult, the steps could involve training yourself to accept the fact that you can actually have this career.

In Chapter 1, you learned about Limiting Beliefs and created a list of some of the ones that you held in the past. As you begin to take action, you will probably start to see some of those self-imposed restrictions try to keep you from moving into your ideal career. The biggest key to overcoming these mental objections is keeping the vision of yourself working in your new career firmly before you. As the objections begin to surface, replace the negativity and doubt with the joy and excitement you feel when you ENVISION yourself in your new career. Once you have put yourself back into the right frame of mind, you can review those doubts more objectively and determine if they are substantial objections, or merely fear finding a voice. Fear is a powerful motivating factor, both for good and for bad. Once you are able to act in spite of your fear, you are on the path to success.

As you begin to ACT, there are three fundamental steps you will follow:

1. Learn about your career.

2. Determine your Escape Date.

3. Identify obstacles and overcome them.

LEARN ABOUT YOUR CAREER

As you start taking steps towards your career, you should learn as much as you can about it. If you plan to open your own business, learn more about your local laws and the licenses that are necessary to start a business. Contact local entrepreneur groups or the Chamber of Commerce, who can help you with the logistics. Find successful people in the same or similar businesses and study their success. Find mentors who can help you along the path.

Most people who truly love their career are happy to talk about it. Many are survivors of previous jobs, so they understand first-hand what it takes to get started in a new career. People who have survived bad jobs know how much happier they are in the right career and they want to help others onto the right path as well. Most successful people do not see newcomers as "competition". That is a mentality of lack. Successful people know we live in an abundant world. There is always room for one more person who is passionate.

It is important that you seek out people who are successful in their careers to provide you guidance. While it may seem obvious, people who are only mediocre or unsuccessful in their field are probably in the wrong line of work. You don't want to spend time learning from someone who would be better off taking their own LEAP! You want to find someone who is obviously passionate about her field and who has become successful. That person is probably in her perfect career.

Many business success gurus have advocated creating a Mastermind group, Board of Directors, or Sounding Board. The concept is to find a group of successful people to help you achieve your goals. The best choices are people who are already successful in the same or related careers. Napoleon Hill's Mastermind Group even included people who he didn't know or who were deceased, but whom he respected and admired. He would ask these "imaginary" group members for help and advice in the same way he asked the real people. And he would usually get the answers he needed because, deep inside, we usually already know the answers. You may have business people who you respect and admire. When you are faced with decisions that are difficult, think about how those people would react.

"Whether you think you can
or think you can't – you're right."

– Henry Ford

CRYSTLE'S STORY

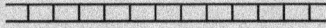

Crystle knew she needed to move beyond envisioning herself with her own shoe business. She could see the business and knew what she wanted to do. It was time to ACT. Crystle had brainstormed and researched the name of her business to make sure that she could get the necessary business licenses in that name. She knew a marketing and branding consultant and worked with him to design a logo and brand elements. Looking online, she found a networking group for entrepreneurs and sought help with completing her business plan. She also spent time doing the fun part – researching what shoes she wanted to carry in her new business.

As the days went by and these small actions started to add up, Crystle moved from having a tiny hope that she could work with shoes to having a business name, product line, business cards, and a brand. In less time than she thought was possible, she was transitioning to her perfect career.

IDENTIFY YOUR ESCAPE DATE

Your Escape Date is the deadline you set for yourself when you will be working in your new career. "A goal is a dream with a deadline," according to Napoleon Hill, and it is important to set a deadline for moving to your new career. By creating a timeline, you shift your thinking from the land of daydreams to the land of concrete reality. When you set your Escape Date, your brain realizes that you meant it when you committed to transitioning to your perfect career. You begin to see the changes more clearly and can focus even more strongly on acting each day to move closer to your new life.

Based on this Escape Date, you can begin to create a schedule of activities that have to happen to enable you to switch careers. This schedule will help you determine when you will take each vital step along the path to your new career.

IDENTIFY OBSTACLES AND OVERCOME THEM

Once you have set your Escape Date, the obstacles will become apparent. You may need training, or money, or contacts in your new career field. Depending on how big a change you are planning, you may need to identify interim steps along the path. You are unlikely to go from the mailroom to the boardroom in one step, so plan out the smaller steps along the way.

Depending on the size of these steps, you may want to create an 'interim' Career Statement. If you are currently working in a job that is unrelated to your perfect career, you may want to set an interim Career Statement that gets you transitioned to the right line of work, then update that interim statement and move towards your final goal within that line of work. The key is to have a Career Statement that is both sufficiently ambitious to keep you motivated and near-term enough that you can see the progress you are making each week.

You will continue to identify obstacles as you move through the steps in your plan. Similarly, you will be continually overcoming those obstacles. As you gain practice overcoming small obstacles, you will gain the confidence to tackle the major ones, knowing that you can overcome those obstacles as well.

Your Mastermind group will help you to identify obstacles. These wise people have walked the path ahead of you and know where they stumbled along the way. Learning from their experiences will smooth your own path to success. Don't be afraid to ask for help from your Mastermind partners. They can save you time and headaches if you use their experiences to help you in your own career transition.

An important first step towards your new career is to live each day as if you already have what you want. In John Maxwell's book *Make Every Day Count*, he says he can determine a person's success by looking at their calendar. How do they spend their time?

Ideally, you will spend time every day making steps towards your goal. Even if the only step you can take on a given day is to read your Career Statement and spend 10 minutes in the morning and evening envisioning yourself in your career, you have still ACTed that day. The next day you can get back on track with finding and overcoming obstacles. If you spend hours every day watching television, then you know you are delaying the achievement of your new career.

The key is to do something every day that brings you a step closer to your goal. Regardless of how small the step may be, it is still a step in the right direction. On some days, you may feel very motivated and can ACT in a big way towards transitioning to your perfect career. By continuing to work towards your career change, you are making it real in your mind. The amazing thing is as soon as you commit yourself 100% to the goal and start moving in that direction, you will find unexpected opportunities coming to you.

"If one advances confidently in the direction
of his dreams, and endeavors to live the life
which he has imagined, he will meet with
success unexpected in common hours."

- Henry David Thoreau

As you commit to your career change, you will discover that new opportunities begin to appear. Synchronicities and coincidences will become normal. Whether those opportunities came up because of your commitment, or you noticed them because of your newfound awareness is irrelevant. You will find options that had not occurred to you before, and these options can lead you further along the path to your dream career.

As you plan your actions, keep in mind that each action should be relatively easy. If you are running up against many obstacles or if you find the tasks very unpleasant, take a hard look at what you are doing and at your goal. If you don't enjoy the process of achieving your dream career, will you truly enjoy working in it? Do not mistake hard work with unpleasantness. You will probably have setbacks and problems in the course of your actions, but you should never feel that you are working *against* anything or anyone. Like any good hike, as you walk the path, you will walk uphill and downhill, but if you feel like you have been hiking a steep path for a long time, then you may want to re-evaluate your chosen career.

The easiest way to tell if you are moving in the right direction is to check your emotions. Do you feel good? Do you feel like you are making progress toward a worthwhile goal? While you may not be actively happy every single day – every life has its ups and downs – you should still be able to feel happy and satisfied about your overall progress. If you do not feel happy, you may need to determine if you are pursuing the right career. Too frequently, people spend their lives fulfilling someone else's dreams – usually their parents' vision of what they should do. Just because your parents decided you should be a doctor or engineer does not mean that you have to follow that path. Living someone else's life will never be as satisfying as living your own life on your own terms.

"But he can't even run his own life,
I'll be damned if he'll run mine!"

– **Jonathan Edwards** in *Sunshine*

If you find yourself not enjoying the career you are pursuing, go back to LEARN and think more about what you truly want. It is important to investigate why you want to accept someone else's vision for your life. For approval? Love? Gratitude? Regardless of the reason, you will find your greatest happiness and greatest sense of fulfillment by finding your own perfect career and living your own life completely.

SETTING DAILY TASKS

The first step towards any dream is the hardest – both to identify the step to take and to make the leap. If you have determined that you need to find a mentor then start making phone calls and doing research in order to find the right mentor. Get your business license started. Sign up for the professional training you need. Sit down and write out a plan with dates to help you to get to your career by your Escape Date. Most people work better under pressure than they do with no end date in mind. Use your Escape Date to create a sense of urgency to make the move to your perfect career.

DOROTHY'S STORY

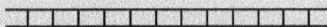

Dorothy set her Escape Date. She had found the school she wanted to attend. It was time to enroll. She took the big step, enrolled in the school and started taking classes. Each day she learned more about her chosen career and loved every minute of it. While she was in school she was also beginning to look for salons and locations to open her business as an esthetician. Dorothy mapped out a business plan and planned for her income changes as she moved from the bi-weekly paycheck of a traditional job to owning her own business. She developed a five-year roadmap for her business.

After her training was complete and she received her certification, Dorothy took another big step, quit the job she didn't like and devoted herself to her new career as an esthetician. She has now been in her perfect career for a few years and is right on track with her five-year plan. Even more importantly, Dorothy still loves her career. She is excited to get up each day and happy to go to work.

As you end each day, one of the last things you should do is review your Career Statement. After you review your Career Statement, write down no more than five things that you plan to do the next day to get you closer to having that career. It's best to target one to three things and make a firm commitment. Then the next morning, get up and do the things on your list. Don't go to bed until you have done the things you planned to do. If you can make this commitment, you cannot fail to achieve your perfect career.

Many people plan the things they wish to achieve in the morning. While that is certainly better than muddling through the day, the best is to plan the night before. That way, while you are sleeping, your unconscious mind can be planning the actions you will have to take during the following day. By waiting until the morning, you miss out on the planning that could be happening while you sleep. Give it a try for at least three weeks and see if you don't get better results from planning the night before rather than planning in the morning. Since you are only planning a few things to do, it shouldn't take much time at all. A 3x5 card is a good planning tool. It's easy to write on, you can carry it with you, and its size keeps you from trying to do too much.

If you fail to plan your day on a regular basis, you need to reconsider whether you are really committed to making a change in your life. It is much easier to talk about change than it is to actually change. By neglecting to do the necessary planning, you are automatically pushing out your Escape Date.

100% commitment requires 100% planning.

YOU WILL RECEIVE WHAT YOU NEED

You will not be given a dream without also being given the means to achieve it. If that means you need more money, then more money will come to you as soon as you open yourself up to receiving it. One of the Limiting Beliefs that most people have is that money is difficult to get and requires hard work.

I believed this for years. What I discovered over time is that money comes easily if you are open to receiving the money. As with any Limiting Belief, you need to evaluate whether you want this in your life. Think about some of the most successful people. Do you think millionaires are working hard at jobs they hate every day? Do you think that hard work is how they earned their millions? Or do you think it was luck? Neither is likely to be true. The hard work was probably a labor of love, requiring more ingenuity than labor, and the luck was far more likely the result of planning, daily action, and unwavering commitment.

ABUNDANCE, SCARCITY, AND RECEIVING THE GOOD

"People are always blaming their circumstances for what they are. I don't believe in circumstances. The people who get on in this world are the people who get up and look for the circumstances they want, and, if they can't find them, make them."

- George Bernard Shaw

I was raised to believe that I had to get a college education and then get a good job to succeed in life. So I did. College was expensive and time consuming, particularly since I couldn't decide on a major. During my four years in college, I drifted from electrical engineering, to medieval studies, to computer technology, to religious studies, to technical writing. That was the first two years. Then I settled on computer science and mathematics, but even that couldn't hold me. I graduated after four years in large part because I was out of money and tired of trying to figure out what I wanted to do with my life.

I had no idea what I wanted to do – what job I wanted to obtain after graduation. But I got through it and eventually got a good job that paid very well. During my years in college, only two things remained constant in my vision of the future – I would live in a large city and work in a cubicle in a large company. Within five years of graduation, I had moved from my town of 60,000 to Portland OR, a city of about two million, and I worked in a cubicle for a very large company – one of its 80,000 employees. Without consciously directing myself, I had still achieved my college dream. I lived in a city and worked at a big corporation.

However, I discovered that working in a cubicle at a big company did not make me feel happy or fulfilled. That was when I started to consciously focus on what I wanted from life. I once read that the important question is not "What do I want out of life" but rather "What can I give to life?" We all know the adage "It's better to give than to receive." It is absolutely accurate.

As long as I focused on what I wanted, I was limited in my success and happiness. Sure, I had managed to get a good job that paid well, but it didn't have the impact that I wanted to have in the world. I was too focused on what I wanted, not what I could offer. Once I focused on what I could give, new pathways of success and joy opened up.

Each day, the actions I took were giving – steps towards helping others. This concept works as well in a corporate job as it does in service professions. Imagine you are in a meeting with several other people. If you focus on what you want out of the meeting, then you are less focused on what you can contribute. Only by focusing on how you can contribute to team success are you going to be able to make the most out of your career. If you are in a service position, the link to success is even more direct. The most successful people in service are always those who look continually for ways to provide better service.

The real key is to recognize that we are all service people; we just have to learn whom we are serving. In some positions, knowing your customer is very straightforward, like the barista who serves lattes at the coffee shop. Less obvious is the office worker or manager, who in fact serves several people - fellow employees, clients, the owner and the shareholders. Knowing whom you serve is just as important as providing good service. As you think about your perfect career, whom will you be serving and how will you provide the highest quality service?

We live in a world focused on lack and scarcity, with the idea that if I have something then you can't have it. However, this is a Limiting Belief. We actually live in a world full of abundance, including an abundance of jobs and career choices. Once you understand this, you can no longer be worried about the unemployment rate. The unemployment rate causes many people to focus on lack and scarcity. "There's no way I can get a good job. The unemployment rate is so high! It will take me forever to find something acceptable." However, the unemployment rate – high or low – doesn't take into account those people who are creating their own futures. By focusing on your perfect career, you are stepping off the unemployment merry-go-round to create a future based on the abundance in the world.

If you focus on scarcity, you will find a lack, a difficulty in obtaining more of anything, because for you to have more, you must take it from someone else. On the other hand if you can learn to focus on abundance, not only do you not have to take from anyone, but your increase can actually be an increase for someone else as well, the proverbial win-win scenario. You will be able to tell if you are on the right path if the actions you take each day are moving you incrementally closer to your goal while simultaneously improving the lives of those around you.

One last word. As you begin to move in the direction of your perfect career, you may start to see other positive changes in your life. The stress and worry from your old job will start to go away. Many people see their personal relationships and health improve as a result of moving towards their perfect career. Money problems can improve, if you stop spending money on "Retail Therapy" to cover up the fact that you hate your job. You might get in touch with your spiritual side, as you clear away the mental clutter and baggage you had from job dissatisfaction. Enjoy these positive changes the same way you enjoy having your perfect career.

EXERCISE:

1. Each evening, write down a list of three to five things that you can ACT on the next day. Do this before you go to sleep so your unconscious mind has an opportunity to do planning while you are asleep. It doesn't matter how big or small each of the items is. What matters is that each and every day you are taking steps to move closer to your perfect career.

2. Review your beliefs about earning money. Do you think that it is hard to earn money? Do you know that money comes from an abundant supply? Go back to Chapter 2 and review the section on Limiting Beliefs and think through how these Limiting Beliefs about money may be holding you back from achieving your perfect career.

3. Continue to review your Career Statement at least twice per day.

4. Keep your thoughts focused on abundance. If your mind begins to sink into a scarcity mindset, immediately refocus on the abundance around you.

Find specific thoughts, images, or music that can help you refocus on abundance. Maybe looking at a picture of piles of money will help you, or listening to a song that expands your thinking. As you look for a mood changer, make sure to choose something that causes positive thoughts. If looking at a pile of money simply makes you feel bad because you lack money right now, then it is not the right image for you. Be sensitive to your own individual needs.

5. Enjoy each day! Know that you are moving in the direction of your perfect career. You are embracing a larger life than most people ever live. While there will likely be delays and setbacks along the way, you can rest assured that you are an active participant in your own life, the star of your own movie.

6. Stay positive. If negative thoughts or fears start to take hold of your mind, take a deep breath and release the thoughts. You are pushing the edges of your Limiting Beliefs each day as you take your steps towards your dream. As you challenge your Limiting Beliefs, you push the edges of your comfort zone. Pushing those edges will likely trigger fears and anxiety. If this happens, pull out your Career Statement and read it several times. ENVISION your career clearly and release your fears, knowing that you are capable and worthy of living a life of abundance.

CHAPTER 5:

POSSESS YOUR PERFECT CAREER

*We must walk consciously only part
way to our goal, and then leap in the dark
towards our success.*

- Henry David Thoreau

5

I am grateful for the idea that has used me.

– Alfred Adler

Congratulations! You've done it! You performed the necessary daily ACTs and now you discover you POSSESS the career you have envisioned for yourself. Celebrate this day! When you POSSESS that which you have worked for, the feelings of happiness should give way to feelings of gratitude. Gratitude is really the final step in any journey.

CELEBRATE EACH STEP ALONG THE WAY

You may be tempted to believe that you will only possess your perfect career on some future day, but that is not true. You truly begin to possess it the day you fully commit yourself to achieving it, the day you LEARN your perfect career and begin to ENVISION your future. Each step you take and each ACT you perform takes you one step closer to POSSESSing your career. Each of those baby steps should fill you with the joy of possession, as you experience the full knowledge that you are on your way to that future. The beauty of pursuing a worthwhile ideal is that you get to experience the joy of possession each day as you come closer to your dream.

This is the joy of possessing. If you don't enjoy possessing each interim step, you likely won't enjoy the end result either. People who do not enjoy medical school likely will not enjoy being doctors. Don't wait until the end of the journey to begin celebrating your success. You became successful the moment you chose to embrace your goal.

One of my favorite motivational works is *The Strangest Secret* by Earl Nightingale. In it, he states "Success is the progressive realization of a worthy ideal." Notice that it is the *progressive* realization. Nightingale acknowledges that each step along the path should be seen as a success, not just the ultimate achievement of the goal. Success isn't a destination; it is a path, and the path consists of the small steps that we make each day. If you are taking the small steps that bring you closer to the ideal career for you, you have been a success from the time you took the very first one.

In the section on ACT, I mentioned that you will know if you are going after the right career because each step along the way will be enjoyable in its own right. If not, then you are on the wrong path. Similarly, a day is unsuccessful if you delay taking the steps towards your perfect career and as unsuccessful days add up, they lead to frustration and lack of purpose. In contrast, successful days will fill you with happiness and a feeling of contribution. Success begets success. Make the successful days far outnumber the unsuccessful days and you will POSSESS your perfect career soon.

GRATITUDE

> *Develop an attitude of gratitude, and give*
> *thanks for everything that happens to you,*
> *knowing that every step forward is a step*
> *toward achieving something bigger and*
> *better than your current situation.*
>
> **– Brian Tracy**

On the day that you POSSESS your ideal career, you should feel the joy and gratitude that are the result of successful hard work. It is possible that some people will attempt to attribute your success to luck. However, you know perfectly well that it was not luck that brought you to this point. It was the culmination of many small ACTs, done day after day, that brought you to this point. It was your focus and determination that brought you to this point. Do not allow others to diminish the effort you have put forth to bring about your success. You deserve full credit for making your perfect career a reality.

To enjoy POSSESSing your perfect career to the maximum extent, cultivate your ability to feel grateful. POSSESS is a state of being; gratitude is a feeling. By feeling gratitude for the success that you have brought into your life, you open yourself up to new opportunities to feel grateful. No one creates his own success in a vacuum. It requires the help and cooperation of others, and they are far more likely to help you if you have been truly grateful for their past assistance.

Think of your own interactions with other people. Who do you like to help the most? Probably someone who needs your help and feels grateful for the help you provide. The ungrateful recipient is less likely to receive future assistance. It's the Golden Rule again: "Do unto others as you would have them do unto you."

Gratitude increases your own joy. If each day you feel the gratitude for all that you have accomplished, gratitude for all of the people who have helped you along the way, and gratitude for the future good that is coming to you, then you will end your day on a very positive note. And you will be open to receiving even more good into your life.

DOROTHY'S STORY

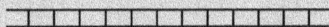

Dorothy knew she hadn't reached the point of having her perfect career without help. She felt grateful for the instructors she had, the unwavering support of friends and family and the guidance she had in LEARNing about her perfect career, ENVISIONing the future, and ACTing each day to finally POSSESS her perfect career. Her gratitude is obvious and it makes others even more likely to try to give her whatever assistance they can.

CRYSTLE'S STORY

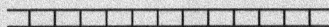

Crystle is still working towards her perfect career. She is a work in progress. However, the fact that she doesn't yet POSSESS that career full-time has not stopped Crystle from feeling grateful for the steps along the way. She feels gratitude to all of the people who have helped her with her business plan, her branding and simple moral support she has received along the way.

Crystle has no doubts that her shoe business is going to be a success. She has ENVISIONED the future, and she knows that it will happen soon. The joy of POSSESSing her perfect career is keeping her motivated as she makes the transition.

EXERCISES:

For at least 15 minutes, sit still and feel the waves of happiness and gratitude for your new, perfect career. Experience the joy of knowing that you now POSSESS your perfect career. You have done what most people only dream about. You have made a major change in your life. You have consciously chosen your own career path.

Look back over the course of your journey to this point. Were there times along the way where you doubted that you would make it through? Were there times when you wanted to give up? Why didn't you? Write down some of the reasons that you were able to get through those dark times. Even though you are currently sitting in the sunshine of POSSESSing your perfect career, there is no guarantee that dark times won't come again. Remembering how you have gotten through these dark times will help if you ever go through them again.

Think of the top two or three people who helped you to reach this point in your career. Once you identify those people, thank them. Express your gratitude, particularly if you haven't done it before. How you express your gratitude is up to you, but give thanks to each of the people who helped you along your way.

It's possible that some of the people who have helped you are no longer a part of your life. If that is the case, you can still give them thanks. Personally, I am grateful on a daily basis for my seventh grade English teacher. Mr. Sheets died many years ago, but that doesn't stop me from acknowledging the enormous impact he had on my life. I was able to directly express that gratitude only once, when I came home from college one summer break. While he did remember me, he had underestimated his influence on me. I think it made his day to realize that he had had such an impact on a student's life.

Find someone who you can help. It doesn't matter how you help them, but give assistance to someone else. By passing along the help, you make an impact in someone else's life. This positive spiral allows everyone to be happier and more productive in their chosen careers.

CHAPTER 6:

STAYING MOTIVATED

Obstacles can't stop you. Problems can't stop you. Most of all, other people can't stop you. Only you can stop you.

– Jeffrey Gitomer

6

Your ability to achieve your dreams depends in large part on how well you handle changes and challenges to your level of motivation. Despite the enthusiasm you have when you first set off to transition to your perfect career, you will likely encounter times when your motivation level drops.

Contrary to what many people think, no one else can *give* you motivation. All motivation comes from within. Lack of motivation usually stems from one of two sources: laziness and fear. Unless you learn to spot the warning signs, these twin enemies can creep up while you aren't looking and drain your motivation completely.

Now everyone goes through productive phases and unproductive phases – times when every day is useful and other times when it is a struggle just to take one step towards your goal. There is no harm in blowing off a little steam now and then doing something frivolous. In fact, sometimes it can be the most productive thing you can do. The hard part is learning to recognize the trends. Are you spending most of your time productively while taking a break every week to watch your favorite TV show? That can be a great way to relieve stress.

However, if days or weeks are going by and you haven't accomplished three things per week, let alone three things per day, you are probably starting to fall into an unproductive cycle. At that point, you need to identify whether the culprit is laziness or fear.

LAZINESS

> *Laziness may appear attractive,*
> *but work gives satisfaction.*

– Anne Frank

So much attention is paid to the aggressive sins, such as violence and cruelty and greed with all their tragic effects, that too little attention is paid to the passive sins, such as apathy and laziness, which in the long run can have a more devastating effect.

– Eleanor Roosevelt

Laziness is both the easiest and the hardest habit to overcome. It takes many forms – watching hours of television at night, aimlessly surfing the Internet, or playing video games. While none of these activities are bad, each can be used to avoid spending time working towards your dream. If you are watching another rerun on TV instead of doing the things you identified to ACT on today, that procrastination could turn the tide of success and kill your motivation. If you allow laziness to keep you from your perfect career, then either you are not going after the right career or your Limiting Beliefs are sabotaging you.

Think about someone you know who really loves their career. Do you think that they would spend hours surfing the Internet instead of doing that job? It's unlikely. They truly love what they do. That passion keeps their interest and motivation high. They can see the progress they are making each day and it keeps them on track to their purpose.

However, laziness may also be a symptom of making too large of a LEAP all at once. You will recall that in the LEARN step, I discussed breaking big Career Statements down into smaller phases. That was because smaller phases help you to stay motivated, because you see the progress you make each day. The laziness you feel could be related to a feeling that you aren't making progress. If so, you can easily recapture the magic you felt by resetting your Career Statement.

STEPS TO CONQUER LAZINESS

1. Identify why you feel lazy. Does it seem like you aren't making progress? Maybe you need to split your Career Statement into phases and work on a small step right now. Success begets success, and as you begin to make those small steps again, you will find your motivation returning.

2. Are you spending a few minutes each day ENVISIONing your future in your perfect career? If you lose sight of why you are putting forth the effort every day, you can easily start to spiral into a lazy haze.

FEAR

*Too many of us are not living our dreams
because we are living our fears.*

– Les Brown

Whereas laziness can be easy to recognize, fear is frequently sneakier. You probably won't even recognize it as fear. You'll start to second-guess whether this career is right for you, thinking, "Do I even want this?" You find yourself focusing more on the potential problems than the joy of success. All of these potential problems stem from fear, which in turn stems from crossing the Terror Barrier. You may recall I introduced the Terror Barrier when I discussed how to ENVISION your future. The Terror Barrier is the set of ideas you have of what is possible and impossible. Getting out of your comfort zone is crossing the Terror Barrier.

Your life is made up of a combination of habits, decisions, and thoughts you have learned from your parents, teachers, friends and associates. Most of your habits you probably don't even recognize, like how you hold your fork and knife or which shoe you put on first. Another habit you have is your feeling of success or failure. Successful people tend to remain successful; failures tend to remain failures. But, situations change. Witness the successful person who loses everything or the failure who makes a fortune. These changes occur because the person changed one habit – how they picture themselves. The successful person who loses everything has usually given in to fear and started making bad decisions, because those decisions are based on fear. The failure who makes a fortune has begun to open his eyes to the possibility of success and invited in, through grateful acknowledgement, the help of those who could provide assistance.

Henry Ford once said, "Whether you think you can or think you can't – you're right." The fear of change can make you think you can't achieve your dreams, as can the crippling fear of failure. These fears come from your current mental programming, your Terror Barrier. While changing that programming is not easy, it can be done. To change negative, limiting programming and fears, follow the same LEAP process.

- LEARN what the fear or limitation is and where it comes from.

- ENVISION yourself free from the fear. Imagine how your life would change.

- ACT every day. Write out affirmations and repeat them daily. Until your new habits form, act as if you already have that new fearless feeling.

- POSSESS your new habit and recognize that you can overcome many limiting habits and beliefs the same way.

I was at a conference where Brian Biro was the featured speaker. Brian is known as the "Breakthrough Coach", and the last segment of his presentation was interactive. He gave each of the attendees a piece of wood, approximately 6 inches by 12 inches and about an inch thick. On one side of the board he had us write our greatest fear. On the opposite side, he had us write what it would mean to us to overcome that fear. On my board, I wrote "Fear of Failure" in large print on one side, and freedom, abundance and happiness on the other side. As a group we were shown how to break a wooden board with one hand. The first person to break a board was a young man in a wheelchair. Despite having limited control over his hands, he smashed through his board with no problem at all. Fifty other people followed, each breaking through their boards and smashing their self-imposed limitations.

The key to breaking through the wooden board is simple. It is focus. You *cannot* focus your eyes on the board. You must focus on the eyes of the person holding the board. You focus *past* the board. By focusing your sight on what lies past the barrier, you can break through quickly. If you let your gaze wander or focus on the board, you just smack your hand and the barrier remains intact.

Out of the whole room of people, I was the last person to break a board. I tried three times and failed. My hand was badly bruised from my efforts. In the three times I had attempted to break through, I felt like I correctly maintained focus past the board, but I was told by many others that at the last possible moment, my eyes would flicker down to the board. My focus was caught by the barrier and by my own fear of failure. On my last chance, with a huge support group around me, I took a deep breath and focused firmly on Brian Biro's eyes as he held the board for me. In one fluid motion, I smashed through the board. It was like the board just melted out of the way. I didn't even feel it with my hand. But I felt it my heart. I let out a whoop of joy, but it was lost in the cries of those around me. The whole group felt the joy of my success, but I knew that I couldn't have done it alone. Not only did I learn the lesson about focus, I also learned the value of a support team.

Several attendees told me afterwards that they remembered my breakthrough moment even more than they remembered their own. Through helping others we help ourselves.

I am a success today because I had a friend
who believed in me and I didn't have the
heart to let him down...

- Abraham Lincoln

Another fear is related to our friends and family. It's a fear of ridicule. Unless you are trying to be a comedian, it's unlikely you want your family and friends to laugh at you. When you start to talk about your career goals to your family and friends, it is likely that they may not be supportive. If your ideal career is very different from what you do now or from your background, well-meaning friends may even try to persuade you that it's a silly idea. The fear of ridicule or of lack of support from those important to you can keep you from achieving your dream. But, are you living your life for yourself or for them? While a support circle can be an important part of achieving success, a circle of friends who are unsupportive may have the opposite effect.

If you are like many people, their lack of support for you and your career goals has far less to do with you and far more to do with them. When you actively pursue your perfect career, it could feel like criticism to others. It may bring into sharp contrast how little they are doing with their own life. When that is the case, their negative reaction is far more related to their own self-criticism than to a lack of support for you.

Be careful not to sound critical of others as you pursue your dream. If you are talking to a coworker and say that you are "leaving this dead-end job and going to get a real career," it may sound like you are being critical of that person's choice to remain in that career. Just remember, what may be the wrong choice for you may be the perfect choice for another person. Be sensitive to the fact that most people do not like their jobs. By stepping out and doing something about your job dissatisfaction, others may feel you are criticizing their job choices.

HOW TO DEAL WITH UNSUPPORTIVE PEOPLE

1. Acquaintances: Do you need to have the person in your life? If the person is a coworker or casual acquaintance, you can simply limit the amount of sharing that you do with him or her. No one is entitled to know your inner most thoughts if you are unwilling to share them.

2. Close friends: Everyone wants their close friends to support their career goals, but it may not always happen. If your friend hates her job, then she may miss getting to share the misery over a drink after work. Your job change could be threatening to your friend if it will cause an income change or cause you to relocate. Jim Rohn said, "You are the average of the five people you spend the most time with." If you make dramatic changes to your life, they, in turn, will cause changes in the lives of others.

3. Family: If the person is your spouse or family member you will have to find a common ground. It may be difficult. The other person may never become a strong supporter, but you should at least be able to have a good relationship. Try to express to others that while you are making changes in your own life, you respect their right to choose their own path as well.

BREAKING DOWN THE BARRIERS

As you reprogram yourself to feel capable and worthy of your dream, you will find that you have fewer and fewer motivational problems. Success breeds success, and as you begin to achieve success – no matter how minor – you will create the internal motivation to continue. Focus on your success and the motivation will follow.

If, however, you begin to focus on setbacks, then your motivation level may drop. If this happens, take a deep breath, sit quietly and ENVISION your life in possession of your goal. Think in detail and for as long as it takes for you to regain the feeling of joy and happiness. Once you feel that joy again, go and do something to take you another step closer to your goal. Taking action will fix that joy in your mind again.

EXERCISES:

1. If you feel your motivation level dropping, try to identify if laziness or fear is causing the problem. Follow the steps in the appropriate section to address the issue.

2. Take time each day to celebrate your successes. Recall how far you have come. By acknowledging every success, you automatically keep motivation high.

3. When your motivation is high, write yourself notes about why you are pursuing your perfect career. List the people whose lives you will impact, including your own. Then read this list when your motivation is low.

CONCLUSION:

TAKE THE LEAP!

By picking up this book and reading it, you've shown you are strongly motivated to make a big change in your professional life. Hopefully you have been following along with the exercises as you have read through this book. If so, you should now be well on your way towards your perfect career. Congratulations!

If you haven't already started to see changes, chances are you will see them soon. The steps that you have worked through in the exercises will have brought clarity to you as you LEARNed what you wanted in your perfect career. The time you spend every day ENVISIONing your new career will help to keep you motivated on a daily basis. The small ACTs that you do every day as you write out the list of three to five things you can do each day will keep you moving in the direction of your perfect career until the day when you POSSESS the career you want.

If you're anything like me, you probably have read the book once and plan to go back through it again, following the steps the second time through. That works too, never fear.

But now that you know what the program is in its entirety, you still have to actually do the exercises if you want the program to work. Just knowing about the steps won't magically get you to your perfect career. You still have to do the work. As you go through the book the second time, you need to spend time working through each step. As you have read the book you have probably been spending some time figuring out what your perfect career is. LEARN is both the hardest and the most critical step in the process. Until you understand what it is that you want out of life, it will be impossible for you to know if you are going in the right direction. Some people seem to be blessed by knowing from the start what the perfect career is for them. For most of us, it's a process of discovery.

The LEAP process will provide you with a step-by-step guide to achieving your perfect career. However, you may find as you make the small steps towards your goal, that something doesn't feel quite right. If that happens to you, go back and re-read the step on LEARN. You may need to tweak to your Career Statement. You may have missed a vital aspect of making your career a perfect fit.

Review the Exercises at the end of the LEARN chapter. As you consider your answers to the questions, think of ways you can modify your Career Statement to more closely match what you want. It may only require a small change. Perhaps you thought you wanted to work at home as a consultant but discover that you miss the busy office environment. You could do a few things to bring that element back into your work life. The most obvious would be to change employers again, to go back to working in a busy office. But that may not be the best option. If interaction with peers is what you miss, join professional groups and make sure to work with others in similar professions. Have lunch with professional contacts on a regular basis. Make sure you do not feel isolated as you make the transition to working at home. If you discover it is the background noise and general feeling of "busy-ness" that you miss, try to find other places where you can work. You might want to rent an Executive Suite if your budget will allow. Shared office space may be another option. And there is always my personal favorite – the neighborhood coffee shop. Spending an hour or two in a lively environment may be just what you need.

SOME DO'S AND DON'TS OF WORKING IN PUBLIC:

If you do decide to spend time at the local coffee shop, do be polite about it.

DO: Buy something from the coffee shop. It could be coffee, tea, or a pastry, but you are using their space (and potentially their Internet connection) so do be a good customer to them as well.

DO: Share the space. If you are alone at a large table, offer to share the space with others who may be looking to do some work. Space may be at a premium.

DO: Leave at some point. While it may be tempting to spend eight hours a day at the coffee shop, unless you are buying drinks all day long you are keeping the shop from getting more business by occupying their space. If you need that much interaction with others, you may need to work in a more traditional office environment.

DON'T: Carry on loud conversations either in person or on a cell phone. Not only are you disturbing others, you may be sharing confidential information in a public space.

DON'T: Spread out over a large area. While you may feel very comfortable at your local hangout, it is someone else's place of business and the coffee shop needs to make money too. If you take up a large area, you are taking more than your fair share. I once went into a local coffee shop where a person who had not only brought in his laptop computer, but also a monitor, keyboard, and mouse, along with a power strip to plug into the wall socket. Leave the monitor at home.

DON'T: Get too comfortable. Sure, one of the benefits of working from home can be working in your pajamas. That doesn't mean that you can wear your pajamas to the coffee shop.

DO: Present a professional image. You don't have to wear a suit to the coffee shop, but neat and tidy is always appropriate.

Whether you hit the bulls-eye on your first try at selecting your perfect career, or if you need a few tweaks to take it from great to perfect, using the LEAP steps allows you to move from doubt to certainty, from unhappiness to joy, and from fear to courage. You grow as a person, grow in your understanding of what you want from your professional life, and grow in your ability to make and accept changes in your life. These skills will serve you in multiple areas.

Now that you are moving in the direction of your perfect career, you will start to see other positive changes in your life. The stress and worry from your old job will start to evaporate. This will frequently mean improvements in other areas of your life. Many people see their personal relationships and health improve as a result of moving towards their perfect career. Money problems can improve, once you stop spending money as an emotional Band-Aid. You might get in touch with your spiritual side as you clear away the mental clutter you had from job dissatisfaction. Embrace the change, but understand that years of having the wrong job will undoubtedly have had a negative impact on you. It will take time, but all of the negative impacts will eventually melt away, leaving you happy, healthy, and productive in your perfect career.

YOUR NEXT LEAP

The beauty of making this one LEAP is that it doesn't have to end there. You can LEAP again. For many people, achieving their perfect career is momentary – it just reveals what the next step should be. It may be that the next step is a minor one, or it could be that the success of your first LEAP allows you to look at a much larger career change. Either way, it is time to start thinking about your next LEAP.

Achieving a goal gives you the confidence and vision to be able to see the next one. An advantage that children of successful parents have is that they can envision a bigger future than most children from disadvantaged backgrounds.

While this is not always true, it's certainly easier to build a strong vision of success when you have a model to follow, than a vision of something you've never experienced. One thing that parents did for me was to give me many diverse experiences. This allowed me to see many different possible futures for myself that I would not have known otherwise. The biggest help for me was actually in ruling out certain paths. I knew things I definitely did not want to do, but I still struggled with what I did want. My parents didn't have the breadth of experience to expose me to everything – few people do. But they gave me the greatest gift of all – curiosity. I read books voraciously and learned about lifestyles that were outside of my direct experience. I learned the spirit of adventure and how to push back fear of change to see the possibility of improvement.

When you have achieved your perfect career, chances are good that you will already have another career step in mind. No career is stagnant, and you should understand that there will always be changes, even if your career seems perfect at the moment. If you have ideas about your next step, go back to the beginning and LEAP again! If you don't have any idea what you want to do next, go back and LEAP again anyway.

Remember those exercises you did during the LEARN step, which helped you discover what you want? Those steps will work again and again. Each time you go through the steps, you will have an easier time making career changes. Setting and achieving goals is a skill, and like any other skill you can improve with practice. You become better at LEARNing what you want; you ENVISION your future more clearly; you form the habit of daily ACTion necessary to POSSESS your goal. All of these skills will enable you to move forward to your next career step even more quickly and easily.

Take the LEAP!